SPORTING 🏆 HEROES

JAMIE VARDY

ROY APPS

ILLUSTRATED BY ALESSANDRO VALDRIGHI

EDGE

FRANKLIN WATTS

LONDON•SYDNEY

Franklin Watts
First published in Great Britain in 2017
by The Watts Publishing Group

Text © Roy Apps 2017
Illustrations © Watts Publishing Group 2017
Cover design: Peter Scoulding
Executive Editor: Adrian Cole

HB ISBN 978 1 4451 5322 3
PB ISBN 978 1 4451 5325 4
Library ebook ISBN 978 1 4451 5324 7

1 3 5 7 9 10 8 6 4 2

Printed in China

Franklin Watts
An imprint of
Hachette Children's Group
Part of The Watts Publishing Group
Carmelite House
50 Victoria Embankment
London EC4Y 0DZ

An Hachette UK Company
www.hachette.co.uk

www.franklinwatts.co.uk

4

THEY DREAM OF PLAYING FOR THEIR TEAM.

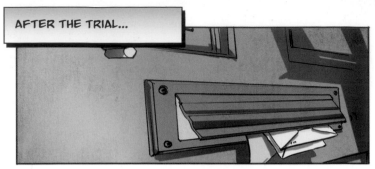

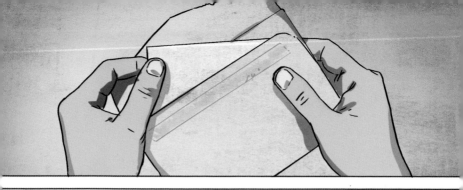

Dear Mr Vardy,
We are pleased to inform you that Jamie
has been selected to join Sheffield Wednesday
Football Club's schoolboy apprentice scheme.

CHAPTER TWO
THE APPRENTICE

'Jamie! Keep the ball closer to your feet. Closer!'

The coach was instructing Jamie how to dribble the ball through a line of cones. Being a schoolboy apprentice wasn't just about playing football matches, there was training to do as well. Dribbling, sprinting, shooting at goal; they were all part of the young footballer's routine.

But Jamie didn't mind. He loved every minute of it. He knew that if he trained hard and played well he would progress through the ranks to the under 14s, then the academy squad, the development squad and finally Sheffield Wednesday's first team.

Over the next few years training got harder and the matches got longer.

Jamie progressed through Sheffield Wednesday's schoolboy squads.

One day at training, the coach came up to him. 'OK, Jamie,' he said, 'I expect you to train especially hard tonight.'

'Why's that?' asked Jamie.

'Because on Saturday you're going to be playing in the academy squad.'

SATURDAY.

I KNOW THESE LADS LOOK BIGGER THAN YOU.

DON'T WORRY, DAD. I CAN HANDLE THEM.

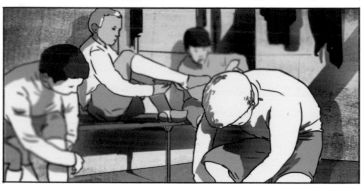

JAMIE USED HIS SPEED TO WEAVE PAST PLAYERS.

At home, Jamie was gloomy and moody. He couldn't hide his disappointment.

'Come on, Jamie,' his step-dad told him, 'you're bound to put on a growth spurt, sooner or later. Then you'll be straight back in the academy team.'

Jamie did get taller, but he didn't get back into the academy team. If he was lucky, he made it onto the subs bench on match day, but he was hardly ever used. The only matches he played were in the younger boys' teams.

When he was sixteen, Jamie and his parents were called into a meeting with the academy squad manager.

'You've trained really hard, Jamie,' the manager told him. 'But it's not been enough. You've got little chance of making it as a pro footballer. I'm sorry, but we're not renewing your contract.'

CHAPTER THREE
THE STEELS

Jamie was heartbroken. His dreams of becoming a professional footballer with the club he'd supported all his life were over.

As the summer drew to a close, it suddenly dawned on him that for the first time in eight years he had no football matches or training to look forward to. He had no job either. He'd left school, thinking he'd still be part of the Sheffield Wednesday set-up.

But Jamie was never one for feeling down for long. He put the academy behind him and got on with his life. After taking some career advice, he enrolled on a sports science course at a college in Rotherham — a nearby town. He made some good friends there.
One day, talking with his mates in the canteen, he let slip that he'd once been on Sheffield Wednesday's books.

17

The Wickersley Youth captain was right. It wasn't long before Jamie was spotted by a local semi-professional side, Stocksbridge Park Steels. He progressed quickly through their ranks, reverting to his role as a striker.

One day, Gary Morrow, the first-team manager, came up to him. 'I've got good news for you,' he said, 'we'd like you to join the first-team squad. You'll get a fee.'

'Yeah?' Jamie said, excitedly. 'How much?'

'Thirty pounds a week,' Gary told him.

By now, Jamie had left college. During the day he worked in a factory, making splints for people with broken legs. All day he stood, leaning over a workbench. It was hard, back-breaking work.

At the end of the season, Jamie found himself playing in a local cup final against a village side. By now, he was beginning to make a bit of a name for himself as a free-scoring striker.

'Their defence will be trying to take you out of the game, Jamie,' Gary Morrow warned him. 'So watch it!'

Jamie was hacked, kicked, shoved and elbowed off the ball. But after each tackle, he got up, dusted himself down and carried on with his marauding runs down the centre.

It was going to take more than a few bruising tackles to stop Jamie Vardy.

CHAPTER FOUR
YOUNG OFFENDER

It was Saturday. It was late — kicking out time for the pubs in Sheffield. Jamie stood outside one of them, chatting with his mates.

A gang of lads came up. They started taunting one of Jamie's mates, who was deaf. Without thinking, Jamie lashed out with his fists and a fight broke out. The police soon arrived and Jamie was arrested. Later, he was convicted of assault and was electronically tagged and placed under curfew for six months.

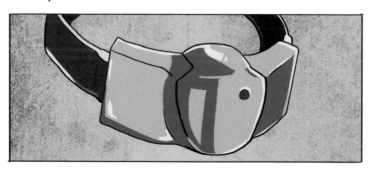

The curfew meant that he had to be off the street and inside at home by six o'clock every evening.

The Stocksbridge Park Steels manager groaned when he heard the news.

'What did you think you were doing, lad?' he asked Jamie, angrily. 'You're meant to be a professional footballer. You're meant to behave responsibly, on the field and off it!' He shrugged. 'I'll have to speak to the chairman, but you could well find yourself out of the door.'

'You can't sack me, I'm your best striker!' Jamie protested.

'And that means striking the ball into the net, not striking another lad on the nose in a pub brawl!' fumed the manager.

In the end, Jamie stayed at Stocksbridge Park Steels. The club chairman rated Jamie's talent as a goalscorer highly enough to want to keep him on.

Nevertheless, the curfew didn't do anything to help Jamie's progress as a footballer. At away matches, he often had to be substituted after an hour or so, just so that he had time to get home by six o'clock.

THE ONLY PEOPLE GLAD TO SEE VARDY LEAVE WERE THE OPPOSITION...

OFF YOU GO, VARDY! IT'S PAST YOUR BEDTIME!

CHAPTER FIVE
THE COD ARMY

Once Jamie had served his sentence and was able to play 90 minutes every week, he soon started to find his scoring touch again.

The fans and players at Stockbridge Steels got used to seeing scouts watching the team play on match days. They knew there was only one player they'd come to see though: Jamie Vardy.

In 2010, Jamie signed for Northern Premier League side FC Halifax Town for a fee of £800. He started at Halifax as if he was still at the Steels, scoring goals every week. By the end of the season he'd bagged 26, and had helped his new club to win the league title!

Soon, the rumours began to spread that Jamie was on his way to a bigger club. Just before he went on holiday to Ibiza, Jamie, always ready with a joke, told the local paper:

In the end, Jamie made a close season move to Fleetwood Town; not quite sunny Ibiza, but at least it was by the sea. His wages were £850 a week.

Fleetwood was once a deep-sea fishing port, and its football team are known as 'the Cod Army'. When Jamie joined them at the start of the 2011—12 season, they were a Conference National side. Jamie Vardy soon changed that. His 31 league goals helped them complete a record-breaking 29 game unbeaten run. They finished the season as Conference National League champions and for the first time in their history were promoted to the Football League proper.

By now, stories about Jamie's goal-scoring exploits had spread nationwide. It could only be a matter of time before a bigger club snapped him up.

There were two very important questions that everyone was asking: which team would come in with a bid for Jamie Vardy, and what would it be worth?

CHAPTER SIX
THE FOXES

It was a big move for Jamie. 'I've played league teams in the FA Cup a few times,' Jamie told the press. 'I think I can manage the step up.'

But Jamie struggled to find form with Leicester. His confidence drained away as the goals dried up. Leicester City fans thought their club had been crazy to spend so much money on a non-league player. At home matches, they made their views on Jamie known:

There may have been a lack of goals in Jamie's life, but there wasn't a lack of money. He was on a very good wage. There was only one thing to do with so much money, Jamie reckoned, and that was to spend it. He would go out of an evening, stay up late, go to bed even later. When it came the next day's training session, he would turn up tired and worn-out.

The club's owner took him to one side. 'The money you have, Jamie. It's not a gift. It's wages. Now go out and earn them.'

Jamie got himself back on track.
He trained hard. But he still struggled
to get into the first team.

He'd sit gloomily on the bench on match days, alongside his mate, a young loanee from Spurs called Harry Kane, who was also struggling to get into the team.

For Jamie, it was like being back at Sheffield Wednesday all over again.

CHAPTER SEVEN
CHAMPIONS!

Jamie stayed at Leicester, and Nigel Pearson was right. He was big for Leicester, scoring 16 goals as the club won the Championship and were promoted to the Premier League.

The start of Leicester's 2014—15 season — their first in the Premier League since 2004 — was mixed. They won one, lost one and drew two. Now, it was time to face the mighty Manchester United.

AT THE KING POWER STADIUM. LEICESTER CITY VS MAN UTD.

WE'RE 64 MINUTES IN AND IT'S 3-3.

LEICESTER COULD BREAK HERE!

THE BALL COMES IN FROM THE RIGHT.

VARDY HAS THE BALL, WITH ONLY DE GEA TO BEAT...

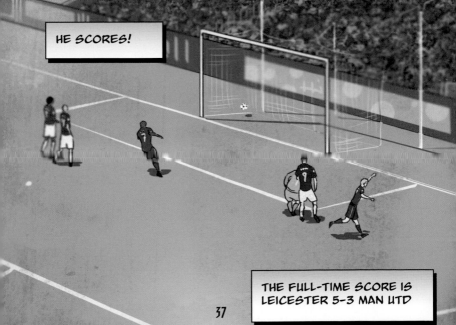

HE SCORES!

THE FULL-TIME SCORE IS LEICESTER 5-3 MAN UTD

Then, it started to go wrong. By April, Leicester were anchored at the bottom of the Premier League, seemingly doomed to relegation.

Jamie had other ideas. Showing blistering form, he scored vital goals that saw Leicester take 22 points from their last nine games. Leicester were safe.

Leicester began the 2015—16 season with a new manager, Claudio Ranieri. He was a big fan of Jamie's skills. 'The way you strike a ball with such power. You're like a cannon!' he told Jamie.

The whole team were enjoying their football; Jamie especially so. At the end of November, he broke Ruud van Nistelrooy's record to become the first player to score in 11 consecutive Premier League matches.

Things were about to get even better for Jamie Vardy. Back on 21st May 2015 he'd been called up to the England squad. His international debut came against the Republic of Ireland, when he replaced Wayne Rooney in the second half. He scored his first England goal in March a year later...

Then, in one of the most extraordinary sporting achievements ever, Leicester City won the 2015—16 Premier League title. They were helped in that astonishing achievement by 24 goals from Jamie Vardy.

A crowd of 240,000 people thronged the streets of Leicester on 16th May 2016. The triumphant Leicester City football team toured the city aboard a fleet of open-top double-decker buses. Waving to the excited fans from the front of the first bus was Jamie Vardy.

The striker had proved all the doubters wrong. The 16-year-old boy had grown up to become a professional footballer. Through hard work and commitment, Jamie had realised his dream — and more! He had become a hero to football fans the world over.

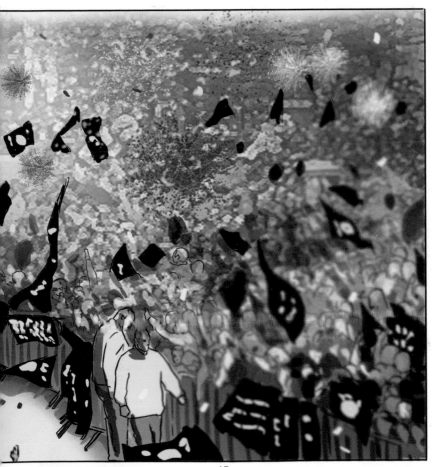

SPORTING 🏆 HEROES

FACT FILE

Full name: Jamie Richard Vardy

Date of birth: 11th January 1987

Place of Birth: Sheffield, England

Height: 1.78m (5ft 8in)

GLOSSARY

consecutive — something that follows in an unbroken pattern, such as winning lots of football matches

curfew — an order forcing someone to stay in their home during set hours, especially at night

form — a measure of how a sportsperson has performed recently

left back — a defender playing on the left side of the pitch

marauding run — in football: a strong, winding movement

relegation — when a football team moves down from one league to a lower league at the end of a season

trial — in football: when players show off their skills in the hope of joining a club

CAREER

Trophies won at FC Halifax Town:

Northern Premier League — Premier Division	2010—11

Trophies won at Fleetwood Town

Conference Premier	2011—12

Trophies won at Leicester City

Football League Championship	2013—14
Premier League	2015—16

Individual Honours

Premier League Player of the Season	2015—16
Footballer Writers' Association Footballer of the Year	2015—16
Premier League Player of the Month	Oct 2015, Nov 2015
Conference Premier Player of the Month	Nov 2011
Conference Premier Top Goalscorer	2011—12

Records

Most consecutive Premier League matches scored in: 11 (29 August 2015 — 28 November 2015)

SPORTING 🏆 HEROES

One day, when Cristiano Ronaldo arrived home from school, he was confronted by Hugo and cousin Nuno...

'You're coming with us, Cris,' said Hugo.

Hugo and Nuno walked off and Cristiano followed after them slowly.

Suddenly, Cristiano knew where they were going ... Andorinha Football Club...

Hugo turned to Cristiano and said: 'You're joining the junior team.'

CONTINUE READING CRISTIANO RONALDO'S AMAZING STORY IN...